for Noah
♥

Conversions

Oven Temperatures

Fahrenheit	Celsius	Gas Mark
275°	135°	1
300°	150°	2
325°	165°	3
350°	175°	4
375°	190°	5
400°	205°	6
425°	220°	7
450°	230°	8
475°	245°	9

US to Metric

cup	tablespoon	teaspoon	metric
1 c	16 tbsp	48 tsp	240 ml
3/4 c	12 tbsp	36 tsp	175 ml
2/3 c	10 tbsp + 2 tsp	32 tsp	160 ml
1/2 c	8 tbsp	24 tsp	120 ml
1/3 c	5 tbsp + 1 tsp	16 tsp	80 ml
1/4 c	4 tbsp	12 tsp	60 ml
1/8 c	2 tbsp	6 tsp	30 ml
1/16 c	1 tbsp	3 tsp	15 ml
--	--	1 tsp	5 ml

Text © 2020 by Danielle Kartes · Illustrations by Annie Wilkinson · Cover and internal design © 2020 by Sourcebooks
Sourcebooks and the colophon are registered trademarks of Sourcebooks. · All rights reserved.
Published by Sourcebooks eXplore, an imprint of Sourcebooks Kids · P.O. Box 4410, Naperville, Illinois 60567–4410
(630) 961-3900 · sourcebookskids.com · Source of Production: Leo Paper, Heshan City, Guangdong Province, China
Date of Production: December 2019 · Run Number: 5016835 · Printed and bound in China. · LEO 10 9 8 7 6 5 4 3 2 1

Little Chef™

Mom and Me
Cooking Together

This book is for

all the special times

between

_____

and

_____

Joyful recipes by Danielle Kartes
Pictures by Annie Wilkinson

SOURCEBOOKS
eXplore

Guess who loves you more than anything in the whole wide world? You guessed it! **YOUR MOM!** Moms, Mamas, and Mommies are silly and brave, beautiful and kind. Your mom is the very best mom for you! She calms your fears. She encourages you to be anything you want to be in this great, big world. You are special because no matter where you go or who you become, your mom will always be right beside you. She works hard to provide for you. She cheers you on from the sidelines and loves you, no matter what. Nothing is as tender or beautiful as your mom's love for you. And moms adore having your help! With this book, you and Mom have a special set of recipes to make just the way you like 'em—delicious! So pull up a chair and start creating memories in the kitchen with the one who loves you so, so much!

Cooking brings out the very best in everyone. When you feed people you love, they feel that love from you! They can see and taste how much you care for them by the way you prepare delicious dishes for them. Good food makes everyone happy! I hope you enjoy spending this time with Mom as you make these fun, simple, joyful recipes.

Follow these **SUPER** important steps to be the **VERY BEST** chef in town!

Listen well to Mom's instructions. Cooking together is fun, but remember that Mom cares for you and knows what's best, so listen close at every step!

Wash your hands. Clean hands make sure that no germy germs or greasy griminess make their way into your food.

Keep a clean workspace. The best chefs pick up all clutter and wipe down the countertops as they work. Ask Mom for a clean, damp dishcloth to get started!

Never touch knives without permission. Mom will be a big help if any food needs to be chopped!

Keep hands and arms away from hot ovens, boiling pots, and sizzling stoves. This way you won't get burned, and it gives Mom a chance to help you by turning the heat up or down!

What's on the Menu?

In this book, you'll find simple, delicious recipes for you and Mom to make together. Each recipe includes ways to personalize it. Do you and Mom love strawberries more than blueberries? No problem! Make pancakes with strawberry syrup. This is your special time together. Use what you love or whatever you have on hand!

Breakfast

Fluffy Lemon and Ricotta Pancakes with Blueberry Syrup

Soft Scrambled Cheesy Eggs

Beverage

Fresh-Squeezed Lemonade

Lunch

Stovetop Mac 'n' Cheese

Veggie Fried Rice

Dinner

Chicken Meatball Sliders (Mini Burgers)

Chicky Tortilla Roll-Ups (Flautas)

Snack

Yogurt and Granola Parfaits

Crunchy Veggies and Buttermilk Ranch Dip

Side

Buttery Steamed Broccoli

Dessert

Double Chocolate, Double Delicious Crackly Top Brownies

Key Lime Pie Milkshakes

Extras

Tips on how to make memories together

Conversation starters and jokes

Celebrate the every day

Write in your own favorite recipes

Making Joyful Memories Together

Cooking along with Mom will help you both to create new and wonderful traditions together! Here are some ways you can make your time in the kitchen special.

♥ Do you like to listen to music? Pick a fun song you and Mom enjoy that can be played each time you cook together.

♥ Try wearing matching aprons, chef's hats, or shirts!

♥ Work together to decide who gets to collect what, who gets to crack the eggs, and who gets to taste test as you cook!

♥ Use a special mixing bowl or spoon that can only be used when you're working in the kitchen together.

♥ Eat your food on fancy dishes (if you want to)!

Want to hear a funny joke?

Why do eggs hate jokes?

Because they always crack up!

What starts with a T, ends with a T, and is full of T?

A teapot.

What is an egg's least favorite day of the week?

Fry-day, of course!

What did the confrontational cake say?

"You want a piece of me?!"

What do you call cheese when it's all by itself?

Provolone.

What does bread wear to bed?

Jammies.

Where do hamburgers go to dance?

The meatball!

Hee-hee!

Ha-ha!

Soft Scrambled Cheesy Eggs

Makes 4 servings Prep time: 5 minutes Cook time: 10 minutes

**Eggs are delicious when you cook them slowly over a low heat!
You and Mom are making the best cheesy eggs you've ever tasted!**

Equipment
Large nonstick skillet
Silicone spatula

Ingredients
1 tablespoon butter
10 eggs
½ cup heavy cream
Salt and pepper to taste
1 cup cheddar cheese,
   shredded

1 Put the skillet on the stove and ask Mom to turn the heat between low and medium. Add the butter and let it get all melty and a little sizzle-y!

2 Crack the eggs into the pan. This can be tricky, but be confident! A quick tap on the countertop cracks the shell just enough for you to push your thumb into the hole and separate the shell into halves. If a shell fragment falls in, it's okay—use a big piece of shell to scoop out the tiny piece.

3 Gently stir with the spatula until the eggs are mixed up, but not fully! You want little ribbons of white through the cooked scramble. Now, add the cream, salt, and pepper. Stir.

4 After about 5 minutes, when the eggs look glossy, sprinkle on the cheese. Cook a minute or two longer, or until they look firm and not runny, with a little shine on top. Smash them on top of toast or even a baked potato!

Add leftover cooked sausage or ham to the pan at the very beginning!

Add some tender young greens such as spinach or arugula.

Some hot sauce at the end is DELICIOUS if you are a spice-lovin' kiddo!

Fresh-Squeezed Lemonade

Makes 1 quart (4 cups) Ⓨ Prep time: 15 minutes

Roll up those sleeves and get ready for the squeeze!

Equipment
2-quart pitcher
Wooden spoon
Citrus squeezer

Ingredients
4 to 6 lemons, juiced
1 cup granulated sugar
3 to 4 cups water

① Wash those lemons with a good rinse under warm water. The warm water loosens up all those juices.

② Squeeze 1 cup of lemon juice using your preferred squeezer, and pour it into your pitcher. Add the sugar and stir until it's dissolved, then add the water. Taste test! Add more water if it's too strong, more sugar if it's too sour, or more lemon juice if it's too sweet! Once it's perfect, enjoy!

Use this same recipe for limeade!

Smash ½ cup of raspberries into the lemon juice and sugar for a raspberry pink lemonade.

Add scoops of vanilla ice cream to your glass for a creamy lemonade float!

Stovetop Mac 'n' Cheese

Makes 4 servings (V) Prep time: 10 minutes (V) Cook time: 10 minutes

No boxed macaroni and cheese over here! I bet you have everything to make this in your refrigerator and pantry! This is as cheesy and simple and yummy as it gets, friend! Wash those hands and pull up a chair!

Equipment

Stockpot
Wooden spoon
Cheese grater

Ingredients

12 ounces dry elbow pasta

8 ounces cheddar cheese, shredded

1 tablespoon butter

1 cup heavy cream

Salt and pepper to taste

1 Have Mom fill the pot with 2 quarts of water and put it on the stove to boil. You will need high heat for this! Cook the pasta according to the package's instructions, or until just soft enough to bite into. This is called *al dente*, from the Italian word for "tooth"!

2 When the noodles are done, ask Mom to drain them. Next, you put the super delicious cheese, butter, and cream into the pot! Careful, the pan is very hot. Now stir, stir, stir! Once it's all melty, it's ready!

Try to use cheddar cheese shredded off the block. Pre-shredded cheese has a powder on it that can make your mac 'n' cheese a little gritty and not so smooth.

Add 1 cup frozen peas along with the cheese.
Add 1 cup leftover chili to make chili mac, or simply add cooked ground beef for a protein-packed lunch.
Serve alongside sliced apples and snap peas for a fun, crunchy, healthy side dish.
Cook fresh broccoli in the same pot as you are cooking the noodles for broccoli mac 'n' cheese.
Use up any other cheese you have on hand. Mozzarella, Parmesan, and Swiss all make lovely additions to the cheddar.

Veggie Fried Rice

Makes 4 servings ⓥ Prep time: 5 minutes ⓥ Cook time: 15 minutes

Equipment

Small bowl
Large nonstick skillet
Wooden spoon

Ingredients

For the Sauce

⅓ cup soy sauce
1 tablespoon brown sugar
1 teaspoon mustard
1 garlic clove, smashed
    and chopped

For the Rice

2 tablespoons olive oil
2½ cups rice, cooked
2 cups veggies of your
    choice (Think carrots
    and onions, snap peas,
    or broccoli. A mixture
    is great! Use what
    you have.)
1 egg

1 Mix up the ingredients for the sauce in a small bowl and set aside.

2 Put the skillet on the stove and have Mom crank the heat up to medium-high. Pour the oil into the pan and let it heat up. Add the rice and veggies. Cook 4 to 5 minutes.

3 Make a well in the center of the rice and crack the egg into the pan, stirring gently but quickly to scramble the egg.

4 Pour the sauce into the rice. Cook 2 to 3 minutes and serve!

Add chopped cucumbers and peanuts at the end for a delightful crunch!

Add 1 cup of any leftover cooked meat you have in the fridge.

Veggies are yummy!

Skip the sauce if you like it plain.

Joyful Moments

When we're together sharing a meal or just having a snack, it's a great time to connect. Here are some questions for you to take turns asking each other to get your conversation going!

♥ If you could be a superhero, what superpower would you have?

♥ What do you like to read about?

♥ What's your favorite memory with Mom so far?

♥ Let's make up a song! What should we sing about?

♥ Who's your best friend? Why?

♥ If you could change anything about yourself, what would it be? Why?

♥ What is the one thing about yourself that you would never change? Why?

♥ What are you thankful for?

♥ If you ruled the world, what would you do first?

♥ You're on a deserted island, and you can only have three toys or games. Which three would you pick?

♥ What's your favorite animal?

♥ What's your favorite pizza topping?

♥ If we could go to the beach today, what would you want to do first?

Chicky Tortilla Roll-Ups (Flautas)

Makes 12 roll-ups 〇 Prep time: 10 minutes 〇 Bake time: 20 minutes

Crispy, creamy, crunchy dinnertime!

Equipment

Baking sheet
Parchment paper
Mixing bowl
Cutting board
Pastry brush

Ingredients

8 ounces cream cheese, softened
½ cup salsa
1 cup cheddar cheese, shredded
1 teaspoon onion powder
1 teaspoon paprika
1 teaspoon garlic powder
Salt and pepper to taste
4 cups chicken, shredded (Rotisserie chicken works amazing!)
12 soft taco-size flour tortillas
4 tablespoons (½ stick) butter, melted

1 Have Mom preheat the oven to 375°F. Line your baking sheet with parchment paper.

2 In your mixing bowl, mix up the cream cheese, salsa, cheddar cheese, seasonings, and salt and pepper until it's all combined. Fold the chicken into the mixture.

3 Put 2 to 3 tablespoons of your chicken mixture in the center of each tortilla and flatten it down on the cutting board. Roll up the tortilla tightly around the filling. It will look like a little flute, also known as a flauta! Place it on your baking sheet seam-side down.

4 Repeat this process until you've rolled up all the tortillas, then brush each one with the melted butter. Bake 25 minutes until they are golden brown and crisp.

Use any meat you love: ground beef, shredded beef, or turkey.

Serve with sour cream, salsa, or guacamole for dipping.

Make a big green salad and chomp on crunchy lettuce alongside your flautas.

Yogurt and Granola Parfaits

Makes 2½ cups granola (4 servings) **Ⓥ** Prep time: 10 minutes **Ⓥ** Bake time: 15 minutes

Equipment
Large mixing bowl
Wooden spoon
Parchment paper
Baking sheet

Ingredients
For the Granola
2¼ cups rolled oats
¼ cup light-tasting oil
   (like canola)
¼ cup brown sugar
1 tablespoon butter, melted
1 teaspoon vanilla
¼ teaspoon ground cinnamon
Pinch of salt

For the Parfait
2 cups yogurt
2 cups fresh berries
Honey for drizzling

1 Okay, little chef, ask Mom to turn the oven on to 350°F. Remember, never touch the oven without Mom's help.

2 Add all the granola ingredients to your large mixing bowl and stir them up! That's it, all done!

3 Now, pour the fresh granola out onto a parchment paper–lined baking sheet. Have Mom put the granola into the oven. Set a timer for 15 minutes. Voila! Your granola is ready! After Mom takes it out of the oven, let it cool until the pan is no longer hot, hot, hot!

4 To make your parfait, put a little yogurt in a bowl or glass and make layers of granola, berries, honey, and more yogurt, if you'd like! Be creative!

For chocolate granola, add 1 tablespoon cocoa powder to the oats.

Sprinkle your granola on top of ice cream for a tasty, sweet crunch!

Add ½ cup sliced almonds for a nutty surprise!

Add the fresh granola to your favorite chocolate chip cookie recipe!

Enjoy your fresh granola with milk for breakfast!

Crunchy Veggies and Buttermilk Ranch Dip

V Makes a little over 1 cup **V**

Have you ever heard of "dump-and-stir" recipes? Simply dump the ingredients in a bowl, stir it up, and you have an easy, yummy dip! Serve with sugar snap peas, carrot sticks, broccoli, or cauliflower florets—or whatever you choose! It's all delicious!

Equipment
Mixing bowl
Fork or whisk for stirring

Ingredients
½ cup mayonnaise
½ cup sour cream
2 to 3 tablespoons buttermilk
½ teaspoon onion powder
½ teaspoon garlic powder
1 teaspoon dried chives
½ teaspoon dried thyme
¼ teaspoon dried rosemary
Salt and pepper to taste
2 to 3 cups of your
    favorite vegetables

1 Put all ingredients except the veggies into a mixing bowl and stir it up. You are now ready to dunk!

Add a little salsa for a kick.

Add a touch of hot sauce for some spice.

Add ¼ cup dill pickle relish and ¼ cup ketchup, and you've got a tasty thousand island dressing for salads or burgers!

Buttery Steamed Broccoli

Makes 4 servings Prep time: 5 minutes Cook time: 6 minutes

These are so fun and simple and look like delicious buttery TREES!

Equipment
Skillet with lid
Spatula

Ingredients
3 cups fresh broccoli florets
2 to 3 tablespoons butter
Salt and pepper to taste

1 Ask Mom to bring one inch of water to a simmer in your skillet over medium-high heat. Add the broccoli and place the lid on the skillet. Set a timer for 6 minutes. Watch those tiny trees turn bright green!

2 Mom will drain any water off after 6 minutes and put the broccoli back inside the hot pan. Cook the broccoli for 1 minute to get ALL the water out. Now, melt the butter into the pan, and they're ready to munch!

Use this recipe for cauliflower too!

Sprinkle ½ cup shredded cheddar cheese over the top of the broccoli for a cheesy delight!

Add a smashed garlic clove to the butter for extra yummy flavor.

CELEBRATE!

Every day can be special. It doesn't have to be a holiday or your birthday—**YOU** are special and that is a reason to celebrate! The best moments in life are often the times we never expected. When we wake up each morning feeling grateful for the day, it gets very easy to have a heart for celebration.

Here are some ways you can celebrate:

Make a pie! Pie is good for every occasion, anytime!

Play a game! Charades, hide-and-seek, tag, you name it! Just be sure to laugh a lot.

Talk to Mom about the foods she loved to eat growing up. Maybe you can make that meal together!

Paint a beautiful picture for someone special to you!

Ask your loved ones if there's anything you can do for them. A generous spirit makes a happy heart!

You are the perfect person to find the joy in the every day. At dinnertime, ask your loved ones what made them laugh today. Did you discover a new way to do something? Share it! Did you try a new food today? What did you think? What little moments stand out? Talk about them at the table.

Key Lime Pie Milkshakes

Makes 4 servings (V) Prep time: 10 minutes

Blender sweets are possibly the most fun dessert EVER!

Equipment

Blender
Rubber spatula or spoon
A medium-size bowl
4 cups
A sweet tooth

Ingredients

1 cup heavy cream
2 tablespoons sugar
½ cup frozen limeade
  concentrate (100% juice)
½ cup half and half
2 cups (1 pint) vanilla
  ice cream
3 whole graham crackers,
  crushed

1 First up, we'll make the blender whipped cream! Pour the heavy cream into your blender and add the sugar. Put the lid on top and ask Mom to help you blend on low for 2 to 3 minutes, or until the cream looks slightly firm. If you turn off the blender, and the cream stays in place, you'll know it's done! Mom will spoon the whipped cream into the bowl.

2 Add the limeade concentrate, half-and-half, and ice cream to the blender and blend on low 1 to 2 minutes.

3 Line up the cups and pour in the milkshake. Top with whipped cream and graham cracker crumbs. DELICIOUS!

Use any flavor of frozen concentrate to change it up.

Add a splash of maraschino cherry juice for cherry limeade!

Make chocolate shakes by using chocolate syrup instead of limeade concentrate!

It's your turn! Make up your own recipe together or write down the recipe for one of Mom's specialties.

Our ♥ Recipe

Date:_____

_____

Serves:_____ Prep Time:_____ Cook Time:_____

Equipment
_____
_____
_____
_____

Ingredients
_____
_____
_____
_____
_____
_____
_____
_____

Directions
_____
_____
_____
_____
_____
_____
_____
_____
_____
_____
_____

Why we love it: _____ ♥